CONTENTS

Photos: Darren Walsh, AP Images, PA Pics.
Produced by Trinity Mirror Sport Media. **Managing Director:** Steve Hanrahan.
Executive Art Editor: Rick Cooke. **Executive Editor:** Paul Dove.
Produced by: Roy Gilfoyle **Design by:** Glen Hind, Ben Renshaw, Jamie Dunmore.
Writer: Richard Godden **Thanks to:** David Antill, Emma Wilkinson, Andy Jones
Printed by: William Gibbons

Trinity Mirror Sport Media

Words | Richard Godden

THAT'S WHY WE'RE CHAMPIONS

The final day of the season was a carnival of celebration for anyone with Chelsea blood running through their veins. After 37 games of a dominant campaign, Sunderland provided the final hurdle to clear... and then it was time to party!

WE ARE TH

CHAMPIONS

Chelsea supporters prepare for an afternoon of celebration

Stamford Bridge, 24.05.15

CHELSEA 3
SUNDERLAND 1

Diego Costa 37 (pen), Remy 70, 88; Fletcher 26

As Chelsea supporters made the familiar, carefree stroll along a sun-kissed Fulham Road to see their heroes in blue crowned champions of England, something felt different.

This wasn't like the first triumph back in 2005, when the emotions had been a mixture of sheer jubilation and disbelief – were we really about to see John Terry lift the Premier League trophy? Nor was it comparable to the last time, in 2010, when our fate was still in the balance going into the final day of the season.

On this occasion there had been an inevitability about our fourth Premier League title after a record 268 consecutive days atop the standings, 21 of which had been accompanied by the sense of accomplishment that comes with achieving the season's lofty goal. Whereas once, in the

words of Suggs, we'd waited so long but we'd wait forever, this time our coronation was long overdue.

That's not to say the 41,620 supporters in attendance, along with thousands more dotted around the various drinking establishments in Fulham, weren't going to savour the moment. That familiar chant of "Champions of England, we know what we are" went up long before kick-off.

In keeping with the tradition of the Blues' west-London home playing host to some of the biggest names in showbiz and sport over the years, One Direction heartthrob Niall Horan was in attendance to see the celebrations unfold from a seat just a few rows behind the manager, while one of the hottest talents in the NFL, JJ Watt of the Houston Texans, flew over from the States to soak up the party atmosphere.

Famous fans Niall Horan (top) and JJ Watt (above) soak up the atmosphere

The heroes of the 2004/05 title-winning team were in attendance and (above) Didier Drogba led the team out

Loïc Remy nets Chelsea's second

Eden Hazard runs at the Sunderland midfield and (right) Juan Cuadrado on the attack

Loïc Remy is congratulated by his team-mates (left) and Diego Costa scored from the spot to equalise for Chelsea

Didier Drogba is carried from the field by his team-mates after his final appearance as a Chelsea player

Moments before kick-off, the noise levels went up another notch with a nod to our first, magical Premier League title success, as the class of 2004/05 were introduced to the crowd on the day a new banner was unveiled in the Matthew Harding Stand: "Players come and go. Legends last forever."

It had added resonance on an afternoon when Didier Drogba would grace the Stamford Bridge pitch for the final time as a Chelsea player. The Ivorian's every touch was cheered from the stands, but there was to be no addition to his 164-goal tally in his 30-minute appearance; only a fitting send-off as those in attendance rose as one to salute a Chelsea great and the captain for the day when he was carried off the pitch by

his team-mates. It would have taken a brave Sunderland player to suggest the referee book Drogba for timewasting!

By this point the Black Cats had taken the lead, but the Blues ended the campaign exactly as we started it, coming from behind to turn a one-goal deficit into a 3-1 win. It was the 24 victories in between, however, which meant this was a day of celebration in west London.

The crowd was hidden awash a sea of blue flags as the players and coaching staff embraced on the playing surface before heading to the dressing room while staff assembled the stage for the presentation we had all been waiting for.

A huge cheer greeted their re-emergence before compere Neil 'Spy' Barnett

introduced them one-by-one as they went up to collect their winners' medals, pausing only to allow the fans to indulge in a hearty rendition of the new terrace favourite: "Fàbregas is magic, he wears a magic hat!" The man himself had even obtained a unique piece of headwear for the occasion.

Then, the moment we had been dreaming of. With everyone in place, the Barclays Premier League trophy was handed over to John Terry by young Chelsea fan Rachel Key, who had been nominated for the honour as a Community Hero by the Chelsea Foundation. With the biggest prize in English football firmly in his grasp, JT hoisted the trophy into the sky and Stamford Bridge erupted. Boy did that feel good.

The fans were out in force as the players received the Barclays Premier League trophy at the end of a brilliant season

The last word, of course, went to Drogba. Addressing the crowd with the crown of the Premier League trophy on his head, the big man paid tribute to those who had helped make his time at the club the most successful in our 110-year history, including Frank Lampard, who was also signing off from English football, albeit in the wrong shade of blue, with a goal for Manchester City.

It was the end of an era for the Blues in one sense, but the overriding feeling was that this was only the beginning. Drogba told his young team-mates they had the potential to be the greatest Chelsea side of them all, a view echoed by José Mourinho shortly after he had concluded the lengthiest of post-season laps of honour by handing over his winners' medal to his daughter and joining the assembled journalists for a glass of Champagne at his post-match press conference.

As much as this day was about celebrating what had been fought for over the past 10 months, it was impossible not to take a tantalising glimpse into what the future may hold. Within two years of our last Premier League title, we were crowned champions of Europe – what odds on Mourinho and his young Blues requiring only half the time?

CHELSEA:
Cech, Ivanovic, Cahill, Terry, Azpilicueta, Mikel (Christensen 78), Matic, Cuadrado (Remy 43), Willian, Hazard, Drogba (Diego Costa 29).
Unused subs: Courtois, Filipe Luis, Boga, Solanke

SUNDERLAND:
Mannone, Jones, Coates, O'Shea, Van Aanholt, Rodwell, Larsson, Johnson (Giaccherini 74), Wickham, Defoe, Fletcher.
Unused subs: Pickford, Reveillere, Graham, Cattermole, Vergini, Buckley

ATTENDANCE: 41,620

Loic Remy scored the final goal of a triumphant campaign to seal a 3-1 win

BARCLAYS PREMIER LEAGUE ⚽ 2014/15

	Team	Pld	HOME					AWAY					GD	Pts
			W	D	L	F	A	W	D	L	F	A		
1	Chelsea	38	15	4	0	36	9	11	5	3	37	23	+41	87
2	Man City	38	14	3	2	44	14	10	4	5	39	24	+45	79
3	Arsenal	38	12	5	2	41	14	10	4	5	30	22	+35	75
4	Man Utd	38	14	2	3	41	15	6	8	5	21	22	+25	70
5	Tottenham	38	10	3	6	31	24	9	4	6	27	29	+5	64
6	Liverpool	38	10	5	4	30	20	8	3	8	22	28	+4	62
7	Southampton	38	11	4	4	37	13	7	2	10	17	20	+21	60
8	Swansea	38	9	5	5	27	22	7	3	9	19	27	-3	56
9	Stoke	38	10	3	6	32	22	5	6	8	16	23	+3	54
10	Crystal Palace	38	6	3	10	21	27	7	6	6	26	24	-4	48
11	Everton	38	7	7	5	27	21	5	4	10	21	29	-2	47
12	West Ham	38	9	4	6	25	18	3	7	9	19	29	-3	47
13	West Brom	38	7	4	8	24	26	4	7	8	14	25	-13	44
14	Leicester	38	7	5	7	28	22	4	3	12	18	33	-9	41
15	Newcastle	38	7	5	7	26	27	3	4	12	14	36	-23	39
16	Sunderland	38	4	8	7	16	27	3	9	7	15	26	-22	38
17	Aston Villa	38	5	6	8	18	25	5	2	12	13	32	-26	38
18	Hull	38	5	5	9	19	24	3	6	10	14	27	-18	35
19	Burnley	38	4	7	8	14	21	3	5	11	14	32	-25	33
20	QPR	38	6	5	8	23	24	2	1	16	19	49	-31	30

WORDS OF WINNERS

This is what some of our champions had to say following our moment of triumph...

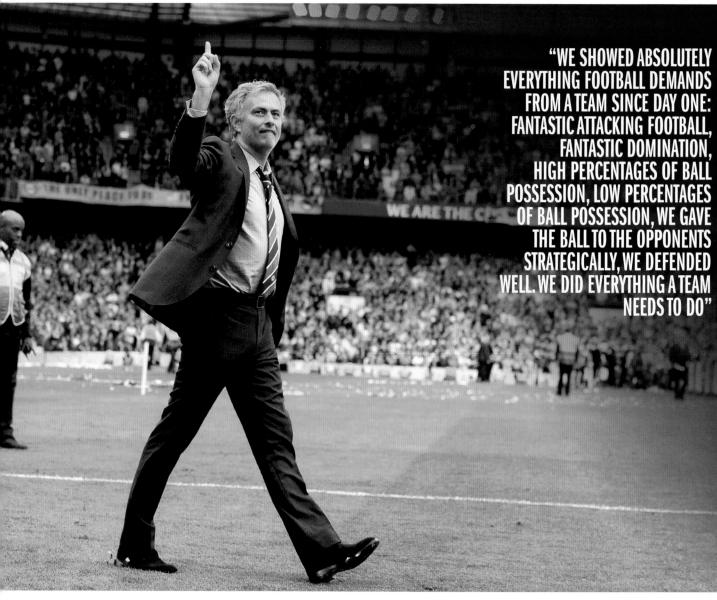

"WE SHOWED ABSOLUTELY EVERYTHING FOOTBALL DEMANDS FROM A TEAM SINCE DAY ONE: FANTASTIC ATTACKING FOOTBALL, FANTASTIC DOMINATION, HIGH PERCENTAGES OF BALL POSSESSION, LOW PERCENTAGES OF BALL POSSESSION, WE GAVE THE BALL TO THE OPPONENTS STRATEGICALLY, WE DEFENDED WELL. WE DID EVERYTHING A TEAM NEEDS TO DO"

JOSE MOURINHO

"The big emotion is when you clinch the title, but when you have the cup in your hand it's always a great feeling. After five years without that at Stamford Bridge it was time for our supporters to enjoy it as well.

"We are champions now but during the season we had some crucial moments we coped with in a fantastic way.

"On 1 January when we were level on points with City after a heavy defeat at Spurs, instead of being a turning point, it was our last defeat before the title was won. The team were always there, everybody knows we deserve it.

"We showed absolutely everything football demands from a team since day one: fantastic attacking football, fantastic domination, high percentages of ball possession, low percentages of ball possession, we gave the ball to the opponents strategically, we defended well. We did everything a team needs to do.

"That's why we are champions and why we deserve to be champions. I think everybody knows that.

"The teams of 2004/05 and 2005/06, and also after that, were fantastic teams. This team is at the beginning, they have won one Capital One Cup and one Premier League, they have to win more to be better than that. You can win something and that's it, or you can win on a regular basis, that's what makes the difference. Let's try to motivate them to do that."

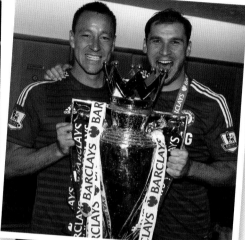

JOHN TERRY

"We've worked so hard this year. The first time you win it is obviously very special but when you go four or five years without winning it and you've grafted all year and you get nothing for it, it really hurts - so we're going to enjoy this.

"I've been a ball boy here, a mascot, I've painted the stadium and this is what I live for, to give the championship to the fans after five years.

"The way we were playing football earlier in the season, after one game Cesc [Fàbregas] came away saying it was the best football he has played, and he has been at Barcelona so for him to say that, everyone listened.

"We played some exciting football but teams make it difficult and it is down to the manager to find a way, and he always does.

"From two days before every game we work on ways to break sides down and get behind them. He has ideas and spends just the right length of time on them.

"He gives you the best opportunity as a player to go into the game fully prepared. You know if you don't play well it is your fault, it's the players' responsibility because he leaves no stone unturned.

"He has a great group of players as well and we and the manager deserve respect for the way we have played this year.

"We have this trophy back and we will look to win it again next season. It is down to these boys to keep winning it again for these fans.

"We've been different class since day one and everyone deserves a pat on the back."

THIBAUT COURTOIS

"Every year is a difficult year with the amount of top teams in this league. We did great this season to win two trophies and, of course, the Premier League is a huge one.

"All the team and myself are really happy and we are looking forward to defending our title next season and achieving some more great things.

"I am very proud because I am 22 years old, nearly 23, and it is an amazing feeling to have already reached that in my career, because it was only a dream to win La Liga title and the Premier League title.

"In England you have four or five contenders for the title and to win it several games before the end of the season is a great feeling."

CHAMPIONS' REACTION

"TO BE TOP OF THE LEAGUE FOR AS LONG AS WE HAVE BEEN IS NOT EASY. WE WORKED TOGETHER AS A TEAM AND THIS IS A REWARD WE ALL DESERVE"

CESAR AZPILICUETA

"It's a very tough league and so to win it is very emotional.

"We have achieved it with the hard work we have put in since we started pre-season in July. To be top of the league for as long as we have been is not easy. We worked together as a team and this is a reward we all deserve."

NEMANJA MATIC

"I feel very proud, we are very happy for the supporters. To be champions you have to be the best team all season. We've shown character and quality.

"We've been in first position since very early. We always feel pressure because we play for a big club, we have to try to win every game, but we've done what we needed to do.

"Every trophy you win is special and after five years, it is a great feeling to have this trophy again. We know how hard we worked for it and that is why we are really enjoying this.

"I think this season we did a great job, we lost only three games in the league and we showed we are a big team.

"Most importantly, we can still improve because we are a young team, with young players and next season I hope that we will improve and play better. I know that it is going to be more difficult for us because next season we play as champions."

21

"WE'VE HAD A LOT OF GREAT PERFORMANCES AND THIS IS JUST THE BEGINNING OF WHAT WE CAN DO FOR THIS CLUB"

BRANISLAV IVANOVIC

"Winning this means a lot. From day one we played very hard, it was difficult, and we are so happy because we dominated this year. We've had a lot of great performances and this is just the beginning of what we can do for this club.

"This season we've had balance in the team. Defensively and offensively we played very well as a team. We didn't concede a lot of goals and we also played attractive football and we dominated all the year.

"Maybe we didn't expect to win it so soon but we definitely deserve it."

"NOW IT IS TIME TO ENJOY IT. IT IS NICE TO FEEL LOVED AND IMPORTANT AND I DO FEEL THAT. I REALLY APPRECIATED ALL THE SUPPORT THROUGH THE SEASON"

CESC FABREGÁS

"It's felt great for a couple of weeks now but to have it in your hands, I think it's a magical moment and hopefully it is the first of many.

"To celebrate with all your team-mates, with the staff, with the fans, it's unbelievable.

"It is a great first season for me, and for the club it has been very successful. Now it is time to enjoy it. It is nice to feel loved and important and I do feel that. I really appreciated all the support through the season."

CHAMPIONS 15

OWN A PIECE OF HISTORY WITH THE CHAMPIONS 15 RANGE

CHELSEA CHAMPIONS BOOK

WRITE YOUR NAME IN CHELSEA HISTORY

Celebrate our inspirational title triumph by
pre-ordering the official Champions 2014/15 book.
Every supporter who pre-orders this fantastic hardback book
will get their name printed on a special fans' Scroll of Honour inside
the publication. Log on to the website below to secure the perfect
personal souvenir of a historic season.
Don't delay – this unique offer is for a limited period only!

ORDER BEFORE 8 JUNE 2015

TO ENSURE YOUR NAME IS IN THE BOOK

CHELSEAMEGASTORE.COM

> "THIS WAS THE ONE THAT I'D NOT WON BEFORE. I'VE BEEN PLAYING IN THE PREMIER LEAGUE FOR A WHILE NOW AND I REALISE HOW HARD IT IS TO WIN THIS. IT FEELS AMAZING. LIKE I SAY, IT'S THE FIRST TIME AND IT FEELS FANTASTIC"

GARY CAHILL

"It's amazing. For the short period that I've been at this club, three-and-a-half years, to win what I've won is tremendous.

"This was the one that I'd not won before. I've been playing in the Premier League for a while now and I realise how hard it is to win this. It feels amazing. Like I say, it's the first time and it feels fantastic.

"He's [José Mourinho] not ashamed or afraid to adapt to every single team that we play, he's so in-depth in terms of the training and the preparation we do for each and every game, it's all different.

"He said in the first year that we weren't quite ready [to win the league] and in the second year we were and obviously he's stuck to his word and done that."

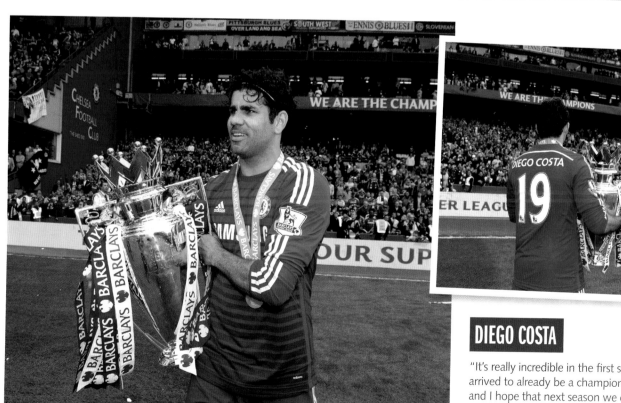

DIEGO COSTA

"It's really incredible in the first season that I arrived to already be a champion. I'm happy and I hope that next season we can do more."

CHAMPIONS' REACTION

"WE DESERVE TO WIN THE LEAGUE BECAUSE WE HAVE HAD TO FIGHT IN EVERY GAME"

LOIC REMY

"The season has been very good because we won two trophies and when I first signed for Chelsea I wanted to win trophies and to improve in every way that I can play.

"For me, I'm very proud of my team first of all and then of my performance. But, of course, next season I want more and more because I'm very ambitious.

"We deserved to win the league because we have had to fight in every game. The Premier League is very difficult and all the players deserve it, even the substitutes and younger players have played very well when they've come in, it's been brilliant.

"I'm really proud because we got two trophies and hopefully next season we will get more."

"WINNING THE LEAGUE WITH CHELSEA WAS WHAT I REALLY WANTED TO ACHIEVE WHEN I CAME BACK AND I THINK I PLAYED ENOUGH GAMES TO GIVE A CONTRIBUTION TO THAT"

DIDIER DROGBA

"It was a strange feeling [being carried off the pitch by his team-mates]. It shows the spirit of this team, the good atmosphere. We are always having fun.

"I wanted to prove to myself that I could come back to the very highest level if possible, play in the Champions League, score in the Champions League. Winning the league with Chelsea was what I really wanted to achieve when I came back and I think I played enough games to give a contribution to that.

"Of course, like every player, you want to play more; you want to play every game. But to be honest when I see all the players we have in this squad, I feel happy playing the number of games I have because I have made a good contribution especially in the last few games."

JOSE MOURINHO

Third title makes it a special Chelsea hat-trick for a special manager

When José Mourinho returned to manage Chelsea for the second time on 3 June 2013 there was a confidence the club could retake our place at the summit of English football – after all, he'd taken us there before.

In 2004/05 and 2005/06 the Portuguese's first two seasons as Chelsea manager resulted in the club becoming Premier League champions, the earlier of those triumphs meaning we'd won the league for the first time in 50 years.

They weren't the only pieces of silverware we collected during a trophy-laden three seasons which saw Mourinho establish himself as one of the game's greatest managers.

His return to SW6 has brought an assuredness, confidence and togetherness to the club that means he can ensure an excellent group of players win the biggest prizes in English football and compete for all the major honours.

When he returned to London two years ago he said: "It was an easy decision [to come back]. I met the boss, the owner and I think in five minutes after a couple of very short but pragmatic questions we decided straight away. I asked the boss 'Do you want me back?' and the boss asked me 'Do you want to come back?' I think in a couple of minutes the decision was made."

For all the fanfare, Mourinho's first season back would be one characterised by rebuilding rather than winning trophies.

A roar that sounded like a goal had been scored greeted him when he emerged from the tunnel before our first game of the 2013/14 season, at home to Hull. He responded by blowing kisses to the crowd,

and the team kept the feel-good factor up with a 2-0 win.

A more competitive league than the one he had left – by his own admission – meant long winning runs proved harder to come by in his first season back, but Mourinho helped keep us top or very close to the top throughout a compelling Premier League campaign.

We would eventually finish four points behind champions Manchester City, but not before Mourinho had masterminded home and away wins against them, as well as second-placed Liverpool. Our victories at the

Etihad and Anfield, against free-scoring sides in excellent form, were prime examples of his tactical acumen.

Though the season ended without silverware, a run to the semi-finals of the Champions League suggested Blues supporters would have much to look forward to in the seasons ahead. And they did not have to wait long to see trophies landing in west London.

First came the Capital One Cup, claimed at Wembley after a 2-0 success against Tottenham.

That merely whetted the appetite for

José Mourinho salutes the crowd before his first game back at Chelsea in August 2013

JOSE MOURINHO

what all Chelsea fans wanted to see most – the return of the Premier League trophy, which was duly captured in May after a dominant campaign which saw us pull away from Manchester City midway through the season and remain top of the table until we couldn't be caught.

Winning the title is a long road but Mourinho added ingredients at the start of the season to a group of players already used to success.

Key men such as Diego Costa and Cesc Fàbregas were brought in, adding goals and class to an already exciting attacking unit.

The squad was also bolstered by full-back Filipe Luis and striker Loic Remy, while club legend Didier Drogba returned as a trusty lieutenant Mourinho knew he could count on.

One of the most significant changes saw on-loan Thibaut Courtois return to the club to play in goal for the majority of the season having impressed everyone in Europe during his spell with Atletico Madrid.

All the components were there and it just needed the right man to put them together and turn them into a well-oiled machine.

Diego Costa made an early impact, embarking on a run of goals that rocketed him to the top of the Premier League goalscoring charts, with Fàbregas pulling the strings behind him as Chelsea made it to the start of December without tasting a single league defeat.

As 2014 turned into 2015, Mourinho's

Mourinho and his skipper, John Terry, lift the Capital One Cup

men were marginally ahead of Manchester City, but the opening months of this year saw them pull ahead of their rivals.

To this point Chelsea had scored notable victories at Anfield and Goodison Park – where the rampant Blues put six past Everton – as well as beating Arsenal, Tottenham and scoring nine goals in the two games against an otherwise impressive Swansea outfit.

The final few months were played out

with consistency and confidence and while our major rivals faltered, Chelsea powered on collecting points with a steely relentlessness.

And so the Premier League trophy returned to Stamford Bridge, the title confirmed with three games still to play.

Very few managers in the world of football can guarantee success but José Mourinho is one of them. And that's why he and Chelsea are made for each other.

Mourinho in reflective mood

MOURINHO'S OTHER CHELSEA TITLES

Frank Lampard celebrates with the fans after scoring the opening goal at Bolton to help Chelsea clinch the title

2004/05

European glory at Porto had thrust Mourinho into the public eye, and when he decided he needed a fresh challenge it was Roman Abramovich's evolving project in west London that caught his attention.

The Portuguese completed his move to Chelsea on 2 June 2004 and there were plenty of fresh faces in the playing squad, too, including defenders Paulo Ferreira and Ricardo Carvalho – who came with him from Porto – and Didier Drogba, a striker who had impressed against Mourinho's former side for Marseille.

Also new to the squad were Petr Cech and Arjen Robben, while John Terry and Frank Lampard were also there to complete the spine of a side that would lose only one league game all season.

The Blues had occasionally gone close in the league in prior years, including in the pre-Abramovich era, so Mourinho's greatest accomplishment in that first glorious campaign was to transform the team and the club into battle-hardened winners who feared no-one and possessed both the ability and the tenacity to cross the line in first place.

In the end, we stormed to the championship title in spectacular fashion, amassing a record 95 points and conceding a paltry 15 goals, the joint-lowest total in English top-flight history.

Mourinho lifts the Premier League trophy for the first time

2005/06

The relentlessness that had marked our success in 2004/05 continued the following year as we won 12 of our first 13 games in all competitions. Another monstrous run of 12 wins in 13 games, and we began the new year 14 points clear at the top.

There were some sticky moments to come, including away defeats to Middlesbrough and Fulham, as well as Champions League and FA Cup exits to new rivals Barcelona and Liverpool respectively, but the Blues motored through those rough patches to claim a second consecutive league title that had long seemed a formality.

It was fitting the title was secured against closest challengers Manchester United at Stamford Bridge – almost a year to the day since we had done likewise at Bolton – as our outstanding form on home turf, where we dropped just two points, was the pillar on which the second championship success was built. Chelsea were again the best team in the land.

A 4-1 win at Anfield was one of the highlights of the 2005/06 season

MOURINHO'S CHELSEA HONOURS

2004/05	2005/06	2014/15	2007

2005	2007	2015	2005

OTHER MAJOR HONOURS

PORTO:
Champions League: 2003/04
UEFA Cup: 2002/03
Primeira Liga: 2002/03, 2003/04
Portuguese Cup: 2002/03
Portuguese Super Cup: 2003

INTER MILAN:
Champions League: 2009/10
Serie A: 2008/09, 2009/10
Coppa Italia: 2009/10
Italian Super Cup: 2008

REAL MADRID:
La Liga: 2011/12
Copa del Rey: 2010/11
Spanish Super Cup: 2012

Didier Drogba and Ricardo Carvalho get the cigars out to celebrate a 3-0 win over Manchester United which sealed the title

GOAL MACHINE

His impact on the Premier League was instant, and for Diego Costa the goals just kept coming

Diego Costa arrived at Chelsea with a big reputation after scoring goals galore in Spain.

There was no way he was likely to sneak under the radar as a surprise package to opposing defenders and managers. He was a star player and everybody knew it. But did he take time to hit the goal trail in a new country? He did not.

Received wisdom suggests it takes foreign footballers weeks, months or years to adjust to the hectic nature of life in the English Premier League.

But then, not all players are Diego Costa.

The Brazil-born striker, who plays international football for Spain, helped Atletico Madrid to the La Liga title and the Champions League final in 2014.

Did he sit back, knowing he could use the cliché about 'taking time to adjust' if the spotlight fell on him for starting his life in England with a barren goalscoring return? Not a chance.

His Premier League introduction went like

this: Burnley (a) one goal; Leicester City (h) one goal; Everton (a) two goals; Swansea City (h) three goals.

That run of seven goals meant he was only the second player in Chelsea history – after Jack Meredith achieved the feat in 1928 – to score in his first four games for the club.

And the goals didn't stop there.

The striker kept adding to his total, meaning he spent the entire season at or around the top of the Premier League goalscoring charts and ended up with 20 in a season which wasn't without its injury problems.

And his contribution to the team isn't limited to his goals output.

Diego Costa is a thorn in the side of any opposition defence. He is good in the air, strong, has excellent close control and has the ability to set up scoring chances for his team-mates.

In whatever way you judge him, he has spearheaded a wonderful Chelsea championship campaign.

DIEGO COSTA - GOAL MACHINE

DIEGO COSTA'S PREMIER LEAGUE GOALS

Burnley (a)	W 3-1	1 goal	1
Leicester City (h)	W 2-0	1 goal	2
Everton (a)	W 6-3	2 goals	3 4
Swansea (h)	W 4-2	3 goals	5 6 7
Aston Villa (h)	W 3-0	1 goal	8
Arsenal (h)	W 2-0	1 goal	9
Liverpool (a)	W 2-1	1 goal	10
West Brom (h)	W 2-0	1 goal	11
Hull City (h)	W 2-0	1 goal	12
West Ham (h)	W 2-0	1 goal	13
Tottenham (a)	L 5-3	1 goal	14
Newcastle United (h)	W 2-0	1 goal	15
Swansea City (a)	W 5-0	2 goals	16 17
Southampton (h)	D 1-1	1 goal	18
Hull City (a)	W 3-2	1 goal	19
Sunderland (h)	W 3-1	1 goal	20

DIEGO COSTA
ON DIEGO COSTA...

"As a striker, obviously you live and get judged by the goals you score. It was good to get off the mark straight away but more than that it is about the team performance and the hard work.

If my first goal didn't come in the first few games I would have still been confident. That is because the team we have is such a great one and the ability of the players that play in midfield and feed the striker is very high, so I always knew goals would come.

Of course it is nice to be the top scorer but when I came here my aim was to win the league. The most important thing is the club going well."

JOHN TERRY
ON DIEGO COSTA...

"Strikers can take months and months [to adapt] but he's scored goals straight away, which is superb, that's great for us.

He's a great character. He gets on great with everyone. He's come to the Premier League to win, he made that clear in pre-season.

I knew he was a very good player but I didn't realise how good until I played against him in the Champions League. He's a real handful and he can play. He can get it, he can turn, he's quick, he's powerful and more importantly he can score goals. He's in the right place at the right time."

DIDIER DROGBA
ON DIEGO COSTA...

"Diego Costa is very good. After coming from a different league, to recreate the same thing he was doing in Spain is fantastic. He is enjoying playing here and being with us and he is the striker we needed this season.

When I look at him I can see the desire to win every challenge and to score goals. He is hungry for goals and that is the best thing for a team like us."

BRANISLAV IVANOVIC
ON DIEGO COSTA...

"He never sleeps in the game, he's not quiet, he wants to be a star, and he wants to be the player around which everything happens in the game.

You can see he is always trying to win duels and look positive on the pitch. He is set up like this for the team, it's his style.

He's a very nice and funny guy. He likes to make jokes."

GIMME FIVE

A handful of the most important games en route to the title

GIMME FIVE

Branislav Ivanovic helped the Blues to race into a two-goal lead after three minutes at Goodison Park

Nemanja Matic grabbed a goal to put Chelsea 4-2 up

SIX SHOOTERS GO GOAL CRAZY

Goodison Park, 30.08.14
EVERTON 3
CHELSEA 6
Mirallas 45, Naismith 69, Eto'o 76; Diego Costa 1, 90, Ivanovic 3, Coleman (og) 67, Matic 74, Ramires 77

An extraordinary Barclays Premier League encounter, including five goals in a frantic 10-minute period in the second half, ended with the Blues running out 6-3 winners on Merseyside.

The tone was set with two Chelsea goals inside the first three minutes, thanks to composed finishes from Diego Costa and Branislav Ivanovic.

Kevin Mirallas struck back for the hosts just before half-time but an own goal from Seamus Coleman restored our two-goal advantage midway through the second period. Further goals were then traded: first Steven Naismith, then Nemanja Matic, before Samuel Eto'o made it 4-3 with almost his first touch for the Toffees.

Ramires hit back instantly and the points were sealed as the clock ticked over to 90 minutes courtesy of the brilliant Diego Costa. He became the first man to score in his first three Chelsea appearances since Adrian Mutu, back in 2003.

Six goals is the most we have scored at Goodison, and the margin of victory matched our previous record wins here, both 3-0 in 1908 and 1956.

EVERTON:
Howard, Coleman, Jagielka, Distin, Baines, McCarthy, Barry, McGeady (Eto'o 70), Naismith, Mirallas, Lukaku (Besic 89). Unused subs: Robles, Alcaraz, Stones, Gibson, Osman

CHELSEA:
Courtois, Ivanovic, Cahill, Terry, Azpilicueta, Ramires, Matic, Willian (Mikel 74), Fàbregas (Drogba 88), Hazard (Filipe Luis 82), Diego Costa. Unused subs: Cech, Zouma, Schürrle, Salah

ATTENDANCE: 39,402

MOURINHO'S VERDICT

"I don't think anybody expects nine goals in a Premier League game between two top-five teams from last season. But they played to win, they played to score, and we played to win, and we played to score. When you have two teams like that lots of goals are possible."

40

Diego Costa grabbed two goals while (right)
Ramires came up with a tremendous finish to
put the result beyond doubt

Loic Remy sealed the points with Chelsea's third goal after Didier Drogba had enjoyed his goalscoring moment with the home fans

DERBY JOY AS RUN GOES ON

Stamford Bridge, 03.12.14
CHELSEA 3
TOTTENHAM HOTSPUR 0
Hazard 19, Drogba 22, Remy 73

Two first-half goals in the space of three minutes, scored by Eden Hazard and Didier Drogba, added to by a Loic Remy strike after the break saw the Blues come out on top in this London derby.

The result preserved our unbeaten start to the campaign and maintained our six-point advantage at the top of the Premier League table.

Tottenham had started the brighter of the two sides and almost took the lead when Harry Kane headed against the bar, but a marvellous piece of individual skill by Hazard gave us the lead, before Drogba extended it shortly after.

Remy, on for Drogba, produced a fine finish 18 minutes from time to compound the visitors' misery and seal a comfortable win.

CHELSEA:
Courtois, Ivanovic, Cahill (Zouma h-t), Terry, Azpilicueta, Fàbregas (Mikel 76), Matic, Willian, Oscar, Hazard, Drogba (Remy 67).
Unused subs: Cech, Filipe Luis, Schürrle, Salah

TOTTENHAM HOTSPUR:
Lloris, Chiriches, Fazio, Vertonghen, Davies, Mason, Bentaleb, Lennon, Lamela, Eriksen, Kane.
Unused subs: Vorm, Naughton, Kaboul, Dier

ATTENDANCE: 41,518

MOURINHO'S VERDICT

"They started better than us and should have scored before us, but after our first goal our team became more stable and confident and we controlled the game. I'm really happy with the points, performance and spirit of the players."

Eden Hazard celebrates putting Chelsea one up against Tottenham

Didier Drogba makes it 2-0

43

Cesc Fàbregas pulled the strings as Chelsea went on a goal spree at the Liberty Stadium

Diego Costa blasts the ball past Lukasz Fabianski to make it 2-0

RAMPANT BLUES SLAY SWANS

Liberty Stadium, 17.01.15
SWANSEA CITY 0
CHELSEA 5
Oscar 1, 36, Diego Costa 20, 34, Schürrle 79

A fine performance in South Wales gave Chelsea our biggest winning margin of this league campaign.

A combination of breathtaking football and Swansea mistakes took the Blues into a 4-0 lead by half-time, with Oscar and Diego Costa sharing the goals. Such was the Chelsea threat that we also hit the woodwork twice in that opening period.

Swansea tightened up their previously open game in the second half and chances were harder to come by, but they couldn't prevent the Blues adding to the score through substitute Andre Schürrle.

The German was on the end of an incisive move that typified much of the play from José Mourinho's men.

Had a Loic Remy shot found its way into the net we would have equalled our best away win in the top flight but five goals was more than enough to put pressure on Manchester City in the title race.

Diego Costa's goals took him on to 17 for the season.

SWANSEA CITY:
Fabianski, Tiendalli, Fernandez, Williams, Taylor, Sigurdsson, Carroll, Dyer (Barrow 74), Oliveira (Fulton 66), Routledge (Emnes 31), Gomis.
Unused subs: Tremmel, Rangel, Bartley, Amat

CHELSEA:
Cech, Ivanovic, Cahill, Terry, Filipe Luis, Fàbregas (Ramires 74), Matic, Willian (Schürrle 76), Oscar, Hazard, Diego Costa (Remy 74).
Unused subs: Courtois, Zouma, Mikel, Salah

ATTENDANCE: 20,785

MOURINHO'S VERDICT

"It was the perfect game. Everything went in our direction. To score in the first minute immediately gives a different game. To be 4-0 up at half-time is not game over, especially in the Premier League, but it's a good situation to control it and we did that in the second half."

Diego Costa and Oscar hit two goals each as Chelsea raced into a 4-0 first-half lead at Swansea

Eden Hazard's moment of real quality made the difference in a tight game against Manchester United

CLASSY BLUES OVERCOME UNITED

Stamford Bridge, 18.04.15

CHELSEA 1
MANCHESTER UNITED 0
Hazard 38

Eden Hazard's 18th goal of the season won a huge game and sent the Blues 10 points clear at the top of the table.

The goal, superbly finished after one of the best moves of the game, came before half-time with Hazard then striking the woodwork not long after it.

From that point on, José Mourinho's men were prepared to allow Manchester United plenty of the ball but the visitors could not find a way through our strong defence. The closest they came was a strike against the outside of the post, after which the threat died away.

"We're top of the league!" rang out around Stamford Bridge shortly before the final whistle blew. The title was now within touching distance.

CHELSEA:
Courtois, Ivanovic, Cahill, Terry, Azpilicueta, Zouma, Matic, Oscar (Ramires 67), Fàbregas (Mikel 90), Hazard (Willian 90), Drogba.
Unused subs: Cech, Filipe Luis, Cuadrado, Solanke

MANCHESTER UNITED:
De Gea, Valencia, Smalling, McNair, Shaw (Blackett 74), Herrera, Mata (Di Maria 70), Rooney, Fellaini, Young (Januzaj 70), Falcao.
Unused subs: Valdes, Rafael, Pereira, Van Persie

ATTENDANCE: 41,422

MOURINHO'S VERDICT

"The team were fantastic. I'm the one that knows how fantastic they were because the game was exactly what we wanted. When you manage to play the game you want to play, it's fantastic. The players were magnificent, on top of that Eden had that magic the top players have, especially in big matches."

Defenders Branislav Ivanovic and (below) John Terry and Gary Cahill enjoy an important win

Eden Hazard heads in (above) and then celebrates the goal that sealed the title

HAZARD CROWNS SUPER SEASON

Stamford Bridge, 03.05.15
CHELSEA 1
CRYSTAL PALACE 0
Hazard 44

Eden Hazard's 19th goal of the season was enough to ensure Chelsea clinched the title with three games to spare and spark scenes of celebration at Stamford Bridge.

Having just been crowned PFA Players' Player of the Year, the Belgian scored on the stroke of half-time after his initial penalty had been saved and from then on, the win was never really in doubt.

Didier Drogba, a man for so many successful seasons, tested the visitors' keeper with a powerful free-kick during the first half in a match which looked like it would be settled by just one goal, and the goal arrived just before the break.

Hazard was felled in the box, took the penalty himself and was on hand to head in the rebound after Julian Speroni had kept out his kick.

Thibaut Courtois was asked to make one decent second-half save but another clean sheet meant it was time to let the party begin – in west London and for Chelsea fans all around the world.

CHELSEA:
Courtois, Ivanovic, Cahill, Terry (c), Azpilicueta, Fabregas, Matic, Cuadrado (Mikel h-t), Willian (Zouma 85), Hazard (Filipe Luis 90), Drogba.
Unused subs: Cech, Ake, Loftus-Cheek, Remy

CRYSTAL PALACE:
Speroni, Mariappa (Kelly 60), Dann, Delaney, Ward, Ledley, McArthur, Puncheon (Sanogo 70), Mutch (Murray 60), Zaha, Bolasie.
Unused subs: Hennessey, Hangeland, Lee, Jedinak

ATTENDANCE: 41,566

MOURINHO'S VERDICT

"What the players are feeling now is fantastic, they deserve it and now they can relax. Palace played like it was a crucial game for them and that was the pure feelings of football."

This is what it feels like to be champions as Branislav Ivanovic (right) and the rest of the team (above) enjoy some triumphant moments in front of the Stamford Bridge crowd after the win against Crystal Palace

Inside the dressing room and on the pitch after the Palace result there was no containing the feeling that a successful Premier League campaign can bring

COMPLETING THE PICTURE

Every moment of the season counts when you're aiming to be champions. Here are the remaining games from a memorable campaign...

Turf Moor, 18.08.14
BURNLEY 1
CHELSEA 3
Arfield 14; Diego Costa 17, Schürrle 21, Ivanovic 34

BURNLEY:
Heaton, Trippier, Duff, Shackell, Mee, Arfield, Marney, Jones, Taylor (Kightly 70), Jutkiewicz (Barnes 70), Ings (Sordell 82). Unused subs: Gilks, Dummigan, Long, Wallace

CHELSEA:
Courtois, Ivanovic, Cahill, Terry, Azpilicueta, Fàbregas, Matic, Schürrle (Willian 77), Oscar (Mikel 82), Hazard (Drogba 83), Diego Costa. Unused subs: Cech, Zouma, Filipe Luis, Torres

ATTENDANCE: 20,699

MOURINHO'S VERDICT

"Everything was fantastic for the second goal: the movement, the quality of the pass, the vision, the understanding between them. It was beautiful."

Diego Costa marked his Chelsea debut with a goal at Burnley while (left) Andre Schürrle rounded off a fantastic move by netting the second

Stamford Bridge, 23.08.14
CHELSEA 2
LEICESTER CITY 0
Diego Costa 62, Hazard 77

CHELSEA:
Courtois, Ivanovic, Cahill, Terry, Azpilicueta, Fàbregas, Matic, Schürrle (Ramires 63), Oscar (Willian 69), Hazard, Diego Costa (Drogba 79).
Unused subs: Cech, Zouma, Filipe Luis, Mikel

LEICESTER CITY:
Schmeichel, De Laet, Morgan, Moore, Konchesky, Mahrez (Albrighton 68), King, Hammond (Taylor-Fletcher 72), Schlupp, Ulloa (Wood 84), Nugent.
Unused subs: Hamer, Hopper, Knockaert, Wasilewski

ATTENDANCE: 41,604

MOURINHO'S VERDICT

"In the second half we were much more aggressive, we won second balls and it was difficult for them. A good, enthusiastic, positive side caused us problems in the first half but in the second we were too strong."

It's that man again...Diego Costa scored the first Stamford Bridge goal of the season while (below) Eden Hazard's strike sealed the victory against Leicester City

Stamford Bridge, 13.09.14
CHELSEA 4
SWANSEA CITY 2
Diego Costa 45, 56, 67, Remy 81;
Terry (og) 11, Shelvey 86

CHELSEA:
Courtois, Ivanovic, Cahill, Terry, Azpilicueta, Fàbregas (Salah 81), Matic, Schürrle (Ramires h-t), Oscar, Hazard, Diego Costa (Remy 72).
Unused subs: Cech, Filipe Luis, Zouma, Willian

SWANSEA CITY:
Fabianski, Rangel, Amat (Fernandez h-t), Williams, Taylor, Ki, Shelvey, Dyer, Sigurdsson, Routledge (Montero 65), Gomis (Bony 75).
Unused subs: Tremmel, Emnes, Tiendalli, Carroll

ATTENDANCE: 41,400

MOURINHO'S VERDICT

"Overall we deserved the victory because we were much better in the second half and we could play the football we want to play, and we could give to the stadium what the stadium was waiting for: a win, and if possible, a win in a beautiful way."

Loic Remy scored his first Chelsea goal against Swansea

A hat-trick from Diego Costa turned the game agaist Swansea City on its head

Etihad Stadium, 21.09.14

MANCHESTER CITY 1
CHELSEA 1

Lampard 85; Schürrle 71

MANCHESTER CITY:
Hart, Zabaleta, Kompany, Mangala, Kolarov (Lampard 78), Milner, Fernandinho (Navas 72), Toure, Silva, Aguero, Dzeko (Sagna 70).
Unused subs: Caballero, Clichy, Demichelis, Nasri

CHELSEA:
Courtois, Ivanovic, Cahill, Terry, Azpilicueta, Fàbregas, Matic, Ramires (Schürrle 62), Willian (Mikel 62), Hazard, Diego Costa (Drogba 85).
Unused subs: Cech, Filipe Luis, Oscar, Remy

ATTENDANCE: 45,602

MOURINHO'S VERDICT

"We came here to a super difficult stadium and a super difficult opponent, and we leave in better conditions than we arrived. It was a very, very good performance."

Andre Schürrle put the Blues ahead at the Etihad Stadium

Oscar waves to the home fans after giving Chelsea the lead against Aston Villa

Stamford Bridge, 27.09.14

CHELSEA 3
ASTON VILLA 0

Oscar 7, Diego Costa 59, Willian 79

CHELSEA:
Courtois, Ivanovic, Cahill, Terry, Azpilicueta, Fàbregas, Matic, Willian, Oscar (Mikel 77), Hazard (Schürrle 68), Diego Costa (Remy 80).
Unused subs: Cech, Zouma, Filipe Luis, Drogba

ASTON VILLA:
Guzan, Hutton, Senderos, Baker, Cissokho, Cleverley, Westwood, Delph, Richardson (Bent 68), Agbonlahor, Weimann (N'Zogbia 68).
Unused subs: Given, Bacuna, Clarke, Sanchez, Grealish

ATTENDANCE: 41,616

MOURINHO'S VERDICT

"The team were very solid and kept control of the game all the time. Even when it was 1-0, I don't remember feeling fear, scared or uncomfortable. The second and third goals obviously killed the game but overall it was a very good performance."

Stamford Bridge, 05.10.14

CHELSEA 2
ARSENAL 0

Hazard 27 (pen), Diego Costa 78

CHELSEA:
Courtois (Cech 24), Ivanovic, Cahill, Terry, Azpilicueta, Fàbregas, Matic, Schürrle (Mikel 69), Oscar (Willian 87), Hazard, Diego Costa.
Unused subs: Zouma, Filipe Luis, Salah, Remy

ARSENAL:
Szczesny, Chambers, Mertesacker, Koscielny, Gibbs, Cazorla (Oxlade-Chamberlain 69), Flamini, Wilshere (Rosicky 82), Ozil, Welbeck, Sanchez (Podolski 78).
Unused subs: Martinez, Monreal, Coquelin, Campbell

ATTENDANCE: 41,607

MOURINHO'S VERDICT

"I'm pleased to win because we played against a good Arsenal. They played a good game and gave us a difficult game. We were able to deal with it without problems, which is fantastic. When we were 1-0 up the game was almost in the pocket."

Diego Costa scored a superb goal to complete victory against Arsenal after (below) Eden Hazard had given the Blues the lead

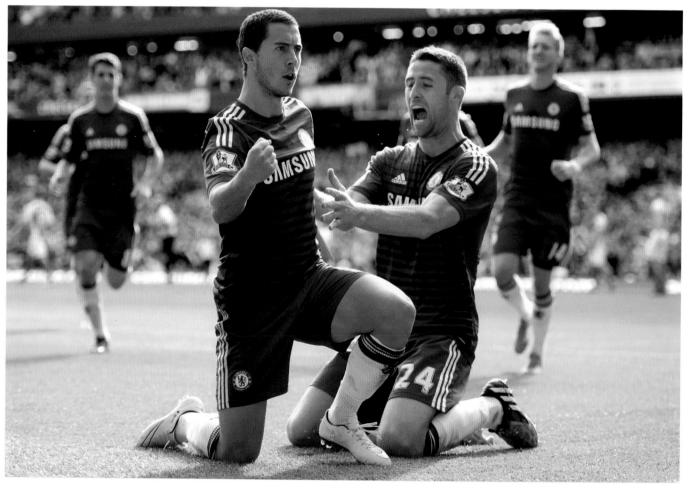

Selhurst Park, 18.10.14

CRYSTAL PALACE 1
CHELSEA 2

Campbell 90; Oscar 6, Fàbregas 51

CRYSTAL PALACE:
Speroni, Kelly, Hangeland, Delaney, Ward, McArthur (Guedioura 68), Jedinak, Ledley (Mariappa 58), Puncheon (Zaha 68), Campbell, Bolasie.
Unused subs: Hennessey, Doyle, Gayle, Chamakh

CHELSEA:
Courtois, Ivanovic, Cahill, Terry, Azpilicueta, Fàbregas, Matic, Willian (Filipe Luis 41), Oscar, Hazard (Salah 86), Remy (Drogba 90).
Unused subs: Cech, Zouma, Mikel, Solanke

ATTENDANCE: 24,451

MOURINHO'S VERDICT

"My team had a fantastic performance. From minute one we did what we wanted to do, have the ball, use the ball and control the game. The second goal was unbelievably good! Against Palace it is never finished until the last seconds. They scored and the situation became dangerous for us."

Cesc Fàbregas completed a fantastic team move by putting us two up against Crystal Palace

Didier Drogba headed Chelsea into the lead at Old Trafford

Old Trafford, 26.10.14

MANCHESTER UNITED 1
CHELSEA 1

Van Persie 90; Drogba 53

MANCHESTER UNITED:
De Gea, Rafael, Smalling, Rojo, Shaw, Blind, Di Maria, Mata (Wilson 67), Fellaini, Januzaj, Van Persie.
Unused subs: Lindegaard, Blackett, Carrick, Fletcher, Herrera, Pereira

CHELSEA:
Courtois, Ivanovic, Cahill, Terry, Filipe Luis, Fàbregas, Matic, Willian (Zouma 90), Oscar (Mikel), Hazard (Schürrle 89), Drogba.
Unused subs: Cech, Ake, Baker, Salah

ATTENDANCE: 75,327

MOURINHO'S VERDICT

"To come here to Old Trafford the way we did – it was fantastic from my boys. This is one of the most dangerous fixtures we've had. The result is not the result we want, but the way we performed means we don't need to look to others."

Stamford Bridge, 01.11.14
CHELSEA 2
QUEENS PARK RANGERS 1
Oscar 32, Hazard 75 (pen); Austin 62

CHELSEA:
Courtois, Ivanovic, Cahill, Terry, Filipe Luis, Fàbregas, Matic, Willian (Drogba 63), Oscar, Hazard (Ramires 90), Diego Costa (Schürrle 77). Unused subs: Cech, Zouma, Ake, Salah

QUEENS PARK RANGERS:
Green, Isla, Dunne, Caulker, Suk-Young, Sandro, Vargas, Henry, Fer (Traore 83), Hoilett (Zamora 60), Austin. Unused subs: Murphy, Hill, Phillips, Kranjcar, Wright-Phillips

ATTENDANCE: 41,486

MOURINHO'S VERDICT

"For 90 minutes Oscar was our best player. Not for the goal, but for the dynamic, for the intensity, for the transitions. He was always sharp."

Oscar gave the Blues a first-half lead against QPR

Anfield, 08.11.14

LIVERPOOL 1
CHELSEA 2

Can 9; Cahill 14, Diego Costa 67

LIVERPOOL:
Mignolet, Johnson, Skrtel, Lovren, Moreno, Henderson, Gerrard, Can (Allen 69), Coutinho (Borini 69), Balotelli (Lambert 79), Sterling.
Unused subs: Jones, Toure, Leiva, Lallana

CHELSEA:
Courtois, Ivanovic, Cahill, Terry, Azpilicueta, Fàbregas, Matic, Ramires (Willian 54), Oscar, Hazard (Filipe Luis 90), Diego Costa (Drogba 89).
Unused Subs: Cech, Zouma, Mikel, Remy

ATTENDANCE: 44,698

MOURINHO'S VERDICT

"My team didn't accept a point as a good result. Obviously it is three important points and a case of when the best team won. A fantastic performance."

Diego Costa attempts a spectacular overhead kick during the win at Anfield. He ultimately proved the matchwinner with a second-half strike after Gary Cahill (above) had equalised during the opening 45 minutes

Stamford Bridge, 22.11.14

CHELSEA 2
WEST BROMWICH ALBION 0
Diego Costa 11, Hazard 25

CHELSEA:
Courtois, Ivanovic, Cahill, Terry, Azpilicueta, Fàbregas, Matic, Willian (Ramires 86), Oscar (Remy 79), Hazard, Diego Costa (Drogba 83).
Unused subs: Cech, Zouma, Filipe Luis, Schürrle.

WEST BROMWICH ALBION:
Foster, Wisdom, Dawson, Lescott, Baird (Gamboa 67), Dorrans (Morrison 83), Gardner, Yacob, Brunt, Sessegnon, Berahino (Anichebe 78).
Unused subs: Myhill, McAuley, Ideye, Samaras

ATTENDANCE: 41,600

MOURINHO'S VERDICT

"The first half was brilliant, beautiful. The quality of our football was high, another dimension. We were playing so well, so fast and fluid. We scored two goals and should have scored more than that, it was fantastic."

Eden Hazard increased the Blues' advantage over West Brom

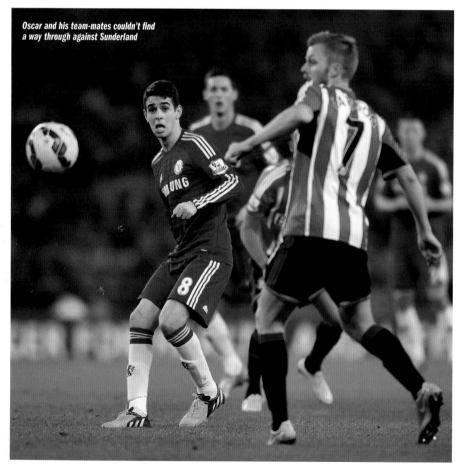

Oscar and his team-mates couldn't find a way through against Sunderland

Stadium of Light, 29.11.14

SUNDERLAND 0
CHELSEA 0

SUNDERLAND:
Pantilimon, Vergini, O'Shea, Brown, Reveillere, Larsson, Cattermole, Rodwell (Gomez 62), Johnson, Fletcher (Altidore 62), Wickham.
Unused subs: Mannone, Bridcutt, Buckley, Coates, Alvarez

CHELSEA:
Courtois, Ivanovic, Cahill, Terry, Azpilicueta, Fàbregas, Matic, Willian (Schürrle 84), Oscar (Remy 76), Hazard, Diego Costa (Drogba 76).
Unused subs: Cech, Filipe Luis, Zouma, Mikel

ATTENDANCE: 45,232

MOURINHO'S VERDICT

"We are not happy with the point but we have to be mature and experienced enough to know in this league every match is difficult. They were playing for a clean sheet and they were successful."

St James' Park, 06.12.14
NEWCASTLE UNITED 2
CHELSEA 1
Cisse 57, 78; Drogba 83

NEWCASTLE UNITED:
Elliot (Alnwick h-t), Janmaat, Taylor, Coloccini, Dummett, Tiote, Colback, Cabella (Cisse 53), Sissoko, Ameobi (Williamson 82), Perez.
Unused subs: Anita, Haidara, Gouffran, Riviere

CHELSEA:
Courtois, Ivanovic, Cahill, Terry, Azpilicueta (Filipe Luis 67), Fàbregas, Mikel, Willian (Drogba 67), Oscar (Schürrle 60), Hazard, Diego Costa.
Unused subs: Cech, Zouma, Ramires, Remy

ATTENDANCE: 52,019

MOURINHO'S VERDICT

"We were unlucky, we didn't score goals when we could have and we conceded the only times they crossed the midfield line, but that's football and I accept it. We were unlucky, that's crystal clear, one day we will be lucky."

Didier Drogba grabbed a consolation as Chelsea tasted defeat for the first time in 2014/15

Diego Costa put the result beyond doubt by netting the second against Hull City

Stamford Bridge, 13.12.14
CHELSEA 2
HULL CITY 0
Hazard 7, Diego Costa 68

CHELSEA:
Cech, Ivanovic, Cahill, Terry, Filipe Luis, Mikel (Ramires 81), Matic, Willian (Schürrle 79), Oscar (Drogba 78), Hazard, Diego Costa.
Unused subs: Schwarzer, Zouma, Azpilicueta, Remy

HULL CITY:
McGregor, Chester, Dawson (Bruce 9), Davies, Elmohamady, Livermore, Huddlestone, Meyler, Robertson, Aluko (Brady 64), Jelavic (Ramirez 74).
Unused subs: Jakupovic, Rosenior, Quinn, Hernandez

ATTENDANCE: 41,626

MOURINHO'S VERDICT

"We didn't play especially well but we played well enough for everybody connected with Chelsea – supporters, players and staff – to be calm, because the game was always under control. We never felt it was at risk."

Britannia Stadium, 22.12.14

STOKE CITY 0
CHELSEA 2
Terry 2, Fàbregas 78

STOKE CITY:
Begovic, Bardsley, Shawcross, Muniesa, Pieters, Nzonzi, Cameron (Adam 68), Walters, Bojan, Arnautovic (Assaidi 81), Crouch (Diouf 63).
Unused subs: Butland, Huth, Whelan, Wilson

CHELSEA:
Courtois, Ivanovic, Cahill, Terry, Azpilicueta, Mikel, Matic, Willian (Schürrle 79), Fàbregas, Hazard (Zouma 90), Diego Costa (Drogba 84).
Unused subs: Cech, Filipe Luis, Ake, Oscar

ATTENDANCE: 27,550

MOURINHO'S VERDICT

"To win here we must play a very good game. We did it because we adapted well to their style of play, when they had the ball. When we had the ball we tried not to lose our identity and play our game."

A vision of joy as Cesc Fàbregas celebrates putting Chelsea two up against Stoke

John Terry's second Premier League goal of the season put the Blues on the road to victory against West Ham

Stamford Bridge, 26.12.14

CHELSEA 2
WEST HAM UNITED 0
Terry 31, Diego Costa 62

CHELSEA:
Courtois, Ivanovic, Cahill, Terry, Azpilicueta, Fàbregas, Matic, Willian (Ramires 85), Oscar (Mikel 82), Hazard, Diego Costa (Drogba 82).
Unused subs: Cech, Zouma, Filipe Luis, Schürrle

WEST HAM UNITED:
Adrian, Jenkinson, Collins, Reid, Cresswell, Kouyate, Noble (Song 59), Nolan, Downing (Amalfitano 74), Carroll (Sakho 59), Valencia.
Unused subs: Jaaskelainen, O'Brien, Jarvis, Cole

ATTENDANCE: 41,598

MOURINHO'S VERDICT

"We played well in two different versions; the first against a defensive side, and we were very good, we moved the ball, there was a good dynamic and lots of chances. In the second half we played against an attacking team. We coped well and found ways to counter-attack."

St Mary's, 28.12.14
SOUTHAMPTON 1
CHELSEA 1
Mane 17; Hazard 45

SOUTHAMPTON:
Forster, Yoshida (Gardos 62), Fonte, Alderweireld, Targett, Wanyama, Schneiderlin, Davis (Long 77), Mane, Tadic (Ward-Prowse 58), Pelle.
Unused subs: Davis, Isgrove, McCarthy, Reed

CHELSEA:
Courtois, Ivanovic, Cahill, Terry, Filipe Luis, Mikel (Drogba 74), Matic, Schürrle (Willian h-t), Fàbregas, Hazard, Diego Costa (Remy 88).
Unused subs: Cech, Zouma, Azpilicueta, Ramires

ATTENDANCE: 31,641

A superb individual goal from Eden Hazard earned a point at Southampton

MOURINHO'S VERDICT

"Southampton defended with everything and they defended a lot. They played with a central defender at right-back, they accumulated a lot of players behind the ball and they did well with their strategy of closing everything. We tried everything and we dominated, we created a lot."

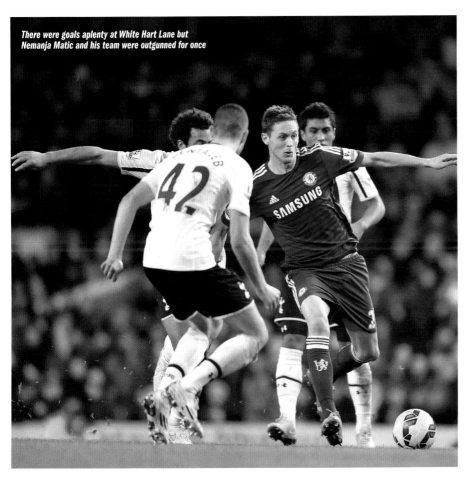

There were goals aplenty at White Hart Lane but Nemanja Matic and his team were outgunned for once

White Hart Lane, 01.01.15
TOTTENHAM HOTSPUR 5
CHELSEA 3
Kane 30, 52, Rose 44, Townsend 45 (pen), Chadli 78;
Diego Costa 18, Hazard 61, Terry 87

TOTTENHAM HOTSPUR:
Lloris, Walker, Fazio, Vertonghen, Rose (Davies 76), Mason (Dembele 13), Bentaleb, Townsend (Paulinho 66), Eriksen, Chadli, Kane.
Unused subs: Vorm, Chiriches, Stambouli, Soldado

CHELSEA:
Courtois, Ivanovic, Cahill, Terry, Azpilicueta, Fàbregas, Matic, Willian (Salah 72), Oscar (Ramires h-t), Hazard, Diego Costa.
Unused subs: Cech, Zouma, Mikel, Drogba, Remy

ATTENDANCE: 35,903

MOURINHO'S VERDICT

"When you concede five goals it's difficult to get a positive result, but in spite of that we scored three and we had chances and lots of initiative to try to score more."

Stamford Bridge, 10.01.15

CHELSEA 2
NEWCASTLE UNITED 0
Oscar 43, Diego Costa 59

CHELSEA:
Cech, Ivanovic, Zouma, Terry, Azpilicueta (Filipe Luis 37), Fábregas, Matic, Willian, Oscar (Ramires 78), Hazard, Diego Costa (Remy 83). Unused subs: Courtois, Cahill, Mikel, Drogba.

NEWCASTLE UNITED:
Krul, Janmaat, Williamson, Coloccini, Dummett, Anita, Colback, Cabella, Sissoko (Riviere 84), Gouffran (Ameobi 63), Perez. Unused subs: Woodman, Santon, Haidara, Vuckic, Armstrong.

ATTENDANCE: 41,612

MOURINHO'S VERDICT

"It's been a difficult period for us – Newcastle, Stoke, Southampton, Tottenham away. We knew it would be very difficult to keep a run of consecutive victories but I think we showed clearly we didn't have a psychological problem with the fact the distance to Man City and Man United was reduced."

The two goalscorers share their elation during the match against Newcastle

Loic Remy gave the Blues the lead against Manchester City

Stamford Bridge, 31.01.15

CHELSEA 1
MANCHESTER CITY 1
Remy 41; Silva 45

CHELSEA:
Courtois, Ivanovic, Zouma, Terry, Azpilicueta, Ramires, Matic, Willian (Drogba 80), Oscar (Loftus-Cheek 90), Hazard, Remy (Cahill 86). Unused subs: Cech, Ake, Christensen, Brown

MANCHESTER CITY:
Hart, Sagna, Kompany, Demichelis, Clichy, Fernando (Lampard 76), Fernandinho, Navas, Silva (Jovetic 89), Milner, Agüero (Dzeko 83). Unused subs: Caballero, Kolarov, Zabaleta, Boyata

ATTENDANCE: 41,620

MOURINHO'S VERDICT

"We are a strong group. The players are a good family. They fight for each other, they stick together. They want to succeed and win and they know the only way to do it is to support each other. The group is really good."

Villa Park, 07.02.15

ASTON VILLA 1
CHELSEA 2

Okore 48; Hazard 8, Ivanovic 66

ASTON VILLA:
Guzan, Hutton, Okore, Clark, Cissokho, Cleverley (Sinclair 73), Westwood, Delph, Gil, Agbonlahor (Benteke 68), Weimann (Cole 79).
Unused subs: Given, Vlaar, Bacuna, Sanchez

CHELSEA:
Courtois, Ivanovic, Cahill, Terry, Azpilicueta, Ramires, Matic, Willian (Cuadrado 79), Oscar (Mikel 73), Hazard, Drogba (Remy 64).
Unused subs: Cech, Zouma, Ake, Loftus-Cheek

ATTENDANCE: 35,969

MOURINHO'S VERDICT

"Apart from the first 15 minutes of the second half we had good control of the game and we showed good ambition after it went to 1-1. Our second goal showed that. The left-back was in the box to cross, and the right-back was in the box to finish. We pushed hard. It was a very important victory."

Branislav Ivanovic's finish against Aston Villa proved he's no ordinary defender

Willian scored a valuable late winner against Everton

Stamford Bridge, 11.02.15

CHELSEA 1
EVERTON 0

Willian 89

CHELSEA:
Cech, Ivanovic, Zouma, Terry, Azpilicueta, Ramires, Matic, Cuadrado (Fábregas 70), Willian (Cahill 90), Hazard, Remy (Drogba 70).
Unused subs: Courtois, Filipe Luis, Ake, Loftus-Cheek

EVERTON:
Howard, Coleman, Stones, Jagielka, Oviedo, Besic (McCarthy h-t), Barry, Lennon (Mirallas 73), Barkley (Gibson 73), Naismith, Lukaku.
Unused subs: Robles, Garbutt, Alcaraz, Kone

ATTENDANCE: 41,592

MOURINHO'S VERDICT

"I don't remember a team that were champions without a couple of victories in the last minute, in my case for sure. Every time I've won a league title I had a couple of matches where I won in the last minute. That was the first time for us this season."

Stamford Bridge, 21.02.15

CHELSEA 1
BURNLEY 1
Ivanovic 14; Mee 81

CHELSEA:
Courtois, Ivanovic, Zouma, Terry, Filipe Luis (Drogba 85), Fàbregas, Matic, Cuadrado (Willian 63), Oscar (Ramires 71), Hazard, Diego Costa.
Unused subs: Cech, Cahill, Azpilicueta, Remy

BURNLEY:
Heaton, Trippier, Keane, Shackell, Mee, Boyd, Arfield, Jones, Kightly (Vokes 78), Ings, Barnes.
Unused subs: Gilks, Duff, Wallace, Reid, Ward, Jutkiewicz

ATTENDANCE: 41,629

MOURINHO'S VERDICT

"'He's adapting [new signing Cuadrado]. He needs to adapt in everything. I truly believe the great player we know we have we are not going to see immediately because the kid needs time to adapt."

Branislav Ivanovic found the net again – this time against Burnley

Eden Hazard's goal earned three points just days after the Capital One Cup final

Upton Park, 04.03.15

WEST HAM UNITED 0
CHELSEA 1
Hazard 22

WEST HAM UNITED:
Adrian, Jenkinson, Tomkins, Reid (Collins 7), Cresswell, Kouyate (Nene 86), Noble, Nolan, Downing, Sakho, Valencia.
Unused subs: Jaaskelainen, O'Brien, Demel, Song, Jarvis

CHELSEA:
Courtois, Ivanovic, Cahill, Terry, Azpilicueta, Zouma, Fàbregas, Ramires, Oscar (Willian 73), Hazard (Remy 90), Diego Costa (Drogba 90).
Unused subs: Cech, Filipe Luis, Loftus-Cheek, Cuadrado

ATTENDANCE: 34,927

MOURINHO'S VERDICT

"West Ham was not the best game to play after a final. Normally you pay a price and West Ham is the best team at playing the way they play, no doubt about it. To cope with it and adapt the way we did defensively is something really difficult to do."

Stamford Bridge, 15.03.15
CHELSEA 1
SOUTHAMPTON 1
Diego Costa 11; Tadic 19 (pen)

CHELSEA:
Courtois, Ivanovic, Cahill, Terry, Azpilicueta, Fàbregas, Matic (Ramires 52), Willian (Cuadrado 83), Oscar (Remy 81), Hazard, Diego Costa.
Unused subs: Cech, Filipe Luis, Zouma, Drogba

SOUTHAMPTON:
Forster; Clyne, Fonte, Alderweireld, Bertrand, Wanyama, Schneiderlin, Mane, Davis (Ward-Prowse 70), Tadic (Djuricic 70), Long (Pelle 82).
Unused subs: Davis, Targett, Gardos, Yoshida

ATTENDANCE: 41,624

MOURINHO'S VERDICT

"In the second half, especially from the moment Ramires came on, we killed their counter-attacks and they felt that, and after that we had complete control of the game. We created lots of chances to win the game but we didn't."

A powerful header from Diego Costa secured a point against Southampton

Chelsea got the better of a five-goal thriller against Hull City

The KC Stadium, 22.03.15
HULL CITY 2
CHELSEA 3
Elmohamady 26, Hernandez 28;
Hazard 2, Diego Costa 9, Remy 77

HULL CITY:
McGregor, Dawson, Bruce, McShane, Elmohamady, Ramirez (Brady 80), Livermore, Meyler (Quinn 80), Robertson (Aluko 80), Hernandez, N'Doye.
Unused subs: Harper, Rosenior, Davies, Sagbo

CHELSEA:
Courtois, Ivanovic, Cahill, Terry, Filipe Luis, Ramires (Oscar 60), Matic, Willian (Zouma 79), Fàbregas, Hazard, Diego Costa (Remy 75).
Unused subs: Cech, Azpilicueta, Loftus-Cheek, Cuadrado

ATTENDANCE: 24,598

MOURINHO'S VERDICT

"If we didn't win the game after the way we played we would have had the same feeling as Southampton. Today by winning we got what we deserved and it's a good feeling."

Stamford Bridge, 04.04.15

CHELSEA 2
STOKE CITY 1
Hazard 39 (pen), Remy 62; Adam 44

CHELSEA:
Courtois, Ivanovic, Cahill, Terry, Azpilicueta, Fàbregas, Matic, Willian, Oscar (Diego Costa h-t) (Drogba 56), Hazard, Remy (Cuadrado 63).
Unused subs: Cech, Filipe Luis, Zouma, Ramires

STOKE CITY:
Begovic, Cameron, Shawcross, Wollscheid, Wilson, Ireland (Crouch 77), Whelan, Nzonzi, Adam (Pieters 77), Walters, Diouf (Arnautovic 63).
Unused subs: Butland, Bardsley, Muniesa, Sidwell

ATTENDANCE: 41,098

MOURINHO'S VERDICT

"We scored the second; we could have scored the third. They had an unbelievable efficiency, scoring one goal from two shots. So the game was difficult, but the important thing was the victory."

Eden Hazard scored from the penalty spot against Stoke, then set up the winner for Loic Remy (below)

Loftus Road, 12.04.15

QUEENS PARK RANGERS 0
CHELSEA 1
Fàbregas 88

QUEENS PARK RANGERS:
Green, Isla (Dunne 90), Onuoha, Caulker, Hill, Phillips, Sandro (Kranjcar 80), Barton, Henry, Austin, Zamora (Hoilett 83).
Unused subs: McCarthy, Mitchell, Comley, Grego-Cox

CHELSEA:
Courtois, Ivanovic, Cahill, Terry, Azpilicueta, Ramires (Oscar 55), Matic, Fàbregas (Zouma 90), Willian (Cuadrado 80), Drogba, Hazard.
Unused subs: Cech, Filipe Luis, Mikel, Brown

ATTENDANCE: 17,939

MOURINHO'S VERDICT

"I'm very happy with my team because we always kept good emotional control, we never lost balance and we were not under pressure. If we had to go home with a point we would have gone home with a point. We were always very stable and we scored at the crucial moment."

A late winner against our west London rivals came courtesy of Cesc Fàbregas

John Terry shows his delight after another important point was earned at Arsenal

Emirates Stadium, 26.04.15

ARSENAL 0
CHELSEA 0

ARSENAL:
Ospina, Bellerin, Koscielny, Mertesacker, Monreal, Coquelin (Welbeck 76), Ramsey, Cazorla, Ozil, Giroud (Walcott 84), Sanchez.
Unused subs: Szczesny, Debuchy, Gibbs, Flamini, Wilshere

CHELSEA:
Courtois, Ivanovic, Cahill, Terry, Azpilicueta, Fàbregas (Zouma 90), Matic, Ramires, Willian (Cuadrado 90+3), Hazard, Oscar (Drogba h/t).
Unused subs: Cech, Filipe Luis, Mikel, Loftus-Cheek

ATTENDANCE: 60,066

MOURINHO'S VERDICT

"John Terry was amazing. He's had fantastic performances in the five or six years we have worked together and some of them with goals. Today everything was clean – his reading of the game, giving cover all around the defensive line, his interceptions with a pass. The team was phenomenal but John was one step ahead of every player."

King Power Stadium, 29.04.15
LEICESTER CITY 1
CHELSEA 3
Albrighton 45; Drogba 48, Terry 79, Ramires 83

LEICESTER CITY:
Schmeichel, Wasilewski, Huth (De Laet 23), Morgan, Albrighton, King (James 18), Drinkwater, Cambiasso, Konchesky, Ulloa, Vardy (Mahrez 77).
Unused subs: Schwarzer, Hammond, Wood, Kramaric

CHELSEA:
Cech, Ivanovic, Cahill, Terry, Azpilicueta, Fàbregas (Mikel 90), Matic, Ramires, Willian (Zouma 83), Hazard (Cuadrado 88), Drogba.
Unused subs: Courtois, Filipe Luis, Ake, Oscar

ATTENDANCE: 32,021

MOURINHO'S VERDICT

"The first half was difficult against a very good team, who were very well organised defensively, who pressed very well and closed spaces. In the second half the early goal was important. After that we were completely in control. We played so well, so fluidly, that the goal had to arrive sooner or later. The boys did fantastically."

Gary Cahill reacts at the final whistle at the King Power Stadium

Stamford Bridge, 10.05.15

CHELSEA 1
LIVERPOOL 1

Terry 5; Gerrard 44

CHELSEA:
Courtois, Ivanovic, Zouma (Cahill 34), Terry, Filipe Luis, Loftus-Cheek (Matic 60), Mikel, Willian, Fàbregas, Hazard, Remy (Cuadrado 83).
Unused subs: Beeney, Azpilicueta, Ake, Drogba

LIVERPOOL:
Mignolet, Can, Skrtel, Lovren, Johnson, Henderson, Gerrard (Lucas 79), Coutinho, Sterling, Lambert (Sinclair 67), Lallana (Ibe 71).
Unused subs: Ward, K Toure, Moreno, Allen

ATTENDANCE: 41,547

MOURINHO'S VERDICT

"We gave them a game and we did what we had to do. In the first half we were by far the better team. Liverpool were more aggressive with the ball in the second half and I think it was a fair result."

John Terry's powerful header put the Blues in front against Liverpool

Isaiah Brown made his debut in a defeat at West Brom

The Hawthorns, 18.05.15

WEST BROMWICH ALBION 3
CHELSEA 0

Berahino 9, 47 (pen), Brunt 60

WEST BROMWICH ALBION:
Myhill, Dawson, McAuley, Olsson, Lescott, McManaman (Gardner 53), Fletcher, Yacob, Morrison (Baird 89), Brunt, Berahino (Ideye 79).
Unused subs: Rose, Wisdom, Mulumbu, Anichebe

CHELSEA:
Courtois, Ivanovic, Cahill, Terry, Filipe Luis, Loftus-Cheek (Ake 72), Matic, Remy (Brown 79), Fàbregas, Hazard, Diego Costa (Cuadrado 63).
Unused subs: Blackman, Azpilicueta, Christensen, Mikel

ATTENDANCE: 24,750

MOURINHO'S VERDICT

"I don't blame the players. When you play since August in the top of your motivation, concentration, commitment, feeling every three days the pressure to win, and then you are champions, you breathe and everything changes. It's difficult to play at that level."

STATS 2014/15

Date	Opposition		Res	Att	Pts	Pos	Formation	Line-up						
August														
Mon 18	Burnley	A	3-1	20,699	3	1	4-2-3-1	Courtois	Ivanovic	Cahill	Terry(c)	Azpilicueta	Fàbregas	Mati
Sat 23	Leicester City	H	2-0	41,604	6	2	4-2-3-1	Courtois	Ivanovic	Cahill	Terry(c)	Azpilicueta	Fàbregas	Mati
Sat 30	Everton	A	6-3	39,402	9	1	4-2-3-1	Courtois	Ivanovic	Cahill	Terry(c)	Azpilicueta	Ramires	Mati
September														
Sat 13	Swansea City	H	4-2	41,400	12	1	4-2-3-1	Courtois	Ivanovic	Cahill	Terry(c)	Azpilicueta	Fàbregas	Mati
Wed 17	Schalke (UCL Group G)	H	1-1	40,648	-	-	4-2-3-1	Courtois	Ivanovic	Cahill	Terry(c)	Filipe Luis	Ramires	Mati
Sun 21	Manchester City	A	1-1	45,602	13	1	4-2-3-1	Courtois	Ivanovic	Cahill	Terry(c)	Azpilicueta	Fàbregas	Mati
Wed 24	Bolton Wanderers (COC3)	H	2-1	40,988	-	-	4-2-3-1	Cech(c)	Azpilicueta	Zouma	Cahill	Filipe Luis	Mikel	Ake
Sat 27	Aston Villa	H	3-0	41,616	16	1	4-2-3-1	Courtois	Ivanovic	Cahill	Terry(c)	Azpilicueta	Fàbregas	Mati
Tue 30	Sporting Lisbon (UCL Group G)	A	1-0	40,734	-	-	4-2-3-1	Courtois	Ivanovic	Cahill	Terry(c)	Filipe Luis	Fàbregas	Mati
October														
Sun 5	Arsenal	H	2-0	41,607	19	1	4-2-3-1	Courtois	Ivanovic	Cahill	Terry(c)	Azpilicueta	Fàbregas	Mati
Sat 18	Crystal Palace	A	2-1	24,451	22	1	4-2-3-1	Courtois	Ivanovic	Cahill	Terry(c)	Azpilicueta (41)	Fàbregas	Mati
Tue 21	Maribor (UCL Group G)	H	6-0	41,126	-	-	4-2-3-1	Cech	Ivanovic	Zouma	Terry(c)	Filipe Luis	Fàbregas	Mati
Sun 26	Manchester United	A	1-1	75,327	23	1	4-2-3-1	Courtois	Ivanovic (90+3)	Cahill	Terry(c)	Filipe Luis	Fàbregas	Mati
Tue 28	Shrewsbury Town (COC4)	A	2-1	10,210	-	-	4-2-3-1	Cech	Christensen	Zouma	Cahill	Filipe Luis	Mikel	Ake
November														
Sat 1	Queens Park Rangers	H	2-1	41,486	26	1	4-2-3-1	Courtois	Ivanovic	Cahill	Terry(c)	Filipe Luis	Fàbregas	Mati
Wed 5	Maribor (UCL Group G)	A	1-1	12,646	-	-	4-2-3-1	Cech	Ivanovic	Zouma	Terry(c)	Filipe Luis	Fàbregas	Mati
Sat 8	Liverpool	A	2-1	44,698	29	1	4-2-3-1	Courtois	Ivanovic	Cahill	Terry(c)	Azpilicueta	Fàbregas	Mati
Sat 22	West Bromwich Albion	H	2-0	41,600	32	1	4-2-3-1	Courtois	Ivanovic	Cahill	Terry(c)	Azpilicueta	Fàbregas	Matic
Tue 25	Schalke (UCL Group G)	A	5-0	54,442	-	-	4-2-3-1	Courtois	Ivanovic	Cahill	Terry(c)	Azpilicueta	Fàbregas	Matic
Sat 29	Sunderland	A	0-0	45,232	33	1	4-2-3-1	Courtois	Ivanovic	Cahill	Terry(c)	Azpilicueta	Fàbregas	Matic
December														
Wed 3	Tottenham Hotspur	H	3-0	41,518	36	1	4-2-3-1	Courtois	Ivanovic	Cahill	Terry(c)	Azpilicueta	Fàbregas	Matic
Sat 6	Newcastle United	A	1-2	52,019	36	1	4-2-3-1	Courtois	Ivanovic	Cahill	Terry(c)	Azpilicueta	Fàbregas	Mikel
Wed 10	Sporting Lisbon (UCL Group G)	H	3-1	41,089	-	-	4-2-3-1	Cech(c)	Azpilicueta	Zouma	Cahill	Filipe Luis	Mikel	Matic
Sat 13	Hull City	H	2-0	41,626	39	1	4-2-3-1	Cech	Ivanovic	Cahill	Terry(c)	Filipe Luis	Mikel	Matic
Tue 16	Derby County (COC QF)	A	3-1	30,639	-	-	4-2-3-1	Cech	Azpilicueta	Zouma	Terry(c)	Filipe Luis	Mikel	Matic
Mon 22	Stoke City	A	2-0	27,550	42	1	4-2-3-1	Courtois	Ivanovic	Cahill	Terry(c)	Azpilicueta	Mikel	Matic
Fri 26	West Ham United	H	2-0	41,598	45	1	4-2-3-1	Courtois	Ivanovic	Cahill	Terry(c)	Azpilicueta	Fàbregas	Matic
Sun 28	Southampton	A	1-1	31,641	46	1	4-2-3-1	Courtois	Ivanovic	Cahill	Terry(c)	Filipe Luis	Mikel	Matic
January														
Thu 1	Tottenham Hotspur	A	3-5	35,903	46	1	4-2-3-1	Courtois	Ivanovic	Cahill	Terry(c)	Azpilicueta	Fàbregas	Matic
Sun 4	Watford (FAC3)	H	3-0	41,010	-	-	4-2-3-1	Cech	Azpilicueta	Zouma	Cahill	Filipe Luis	Ramires	Mikel
Sat 10	Newcastle United	H	2-0	41,612	49	1	4-2-3-1	Cech	Ivanovic	Zouma	Terry(c)	Azpilicueta	Fàbregas	Matic
Sat 17	Swansea City	A	5-0	20,785	52	1	4-2-3-1	Cech	Ivanovic	Cahill	Terry(c)	Filipe Luis	Fàbregas	Matic
Tue 20	Liverpool (COC SF, 1st leg)	A	1-1	44,573	-	-	4-2-3-1	Courtois	Ivanovic	Cahill	Terry(c)	Filipe Luis	Mikel	Matic
Sat 24	Bradford City (FAC4)	H	2-4	41,014	-	-	4-2-3-1	Cech	Christensen	Zouma	Cahill	Azpilicueta	Ramires	Mikel
Tue 27	Liverpool (COC SF, 2nd leg)	H	1-0*	40,659	-	-	4-2-3-1	Courtois	Ivanovic	Zouma	Terry(c)	Filipe Luis	Fàbregas	Matic
Sat 31	Manchester City	H	1-1	41,620	53	1	4-2-3-1	Courtois	Ivanovic	Zouma	Terry(c)	Azpilicueta	Ramires	Matic
February														
Sat 7	Aston Villa	A	2-1	35,969	56	1	4-2-3-1	Courtois	Ivanovic	Cahill	Terry(c)	Azpilicueta	Ramires	Matic
Wed 11	Everton	H	1-0	41,592	59	1	4-2-3-1	Cech	Ivanovic	Zouma	Terry(c)	Azpilicueta	Ramires	Matic
Tue 17	Paris Saint-Germain (UCL Rd of 16, 1st leg)	A	1-1	46,146	-	-	4-2-3-1	Courtois	Ivanovic	Cahill	Terry(c)	Azpilicueta	Ramires	Matic
Sat 21	Burnley	H	1-1	41,629	60	1	4-2-3-1	Courtois	Ivanovic	Zouma	Terry(c)	Filipe Luis	Fàbregas	Matic
March														
Sun 1	Tottenham Hotspur (COC final)	N	2-0	89,297	-	-	4-3-3	Cech	Ivanovic	Cahill	Terry(c)	Azpilicueta	Ramires	Zoum
Wed 4	West Ham United	A	1-0	34,927	63	1	4-2-3-1	Courtois	Ivanovic	Cahill	Terry(c)	Azpilicueta	Zouma	Fàbre
Wed 11	Paris Saint-Germain (UCL Rd of 16, 2nd leg)	H	2-2•	37,692	-	-	4-2-3-1	Courtois	Ivanovic	Cahill	Terry(c)	Azpilicueta	Fàbregas	Matic
Sun 15	Southampton	H	1-1	41,624	64	1	4-2-3-1	Courtois	Ivanovic	Cahill	Terry(c)	Azpilicueta	Fàbregas	Matic
Sun 22	Hull City	A	3-2	24,598	67	1	4-2-3-1	Courtois	Ivanovic	Cahill	Terry(c)	Filipe Luis	Ramires	Matic
April														
Sat 4	Stoke City	H	2-1	41,098	70	1	4-2-3-1	Courtois	Ivanovic	Cahill	Terry(c)	Azpilicueta	Fàbregas	Matic
Sun 12	Queens Park Rangers	A	1-0	17,939	73	1	4-3-3	Courtois	Ivanovic	Cahill	Terry(c)	Azpilicueta	Ramires	Matic
Sat 18	Manchester United	H	1-0	41,422	76	1	4-2-3-1	Courtois	Ivanovic	Cahill	Terry(c)	Azpilicueta	Ramires	Matic
Sun 26	Arsenal	A	0-0	60,066	77	1	4-2-3-1	Courtois	Ivanovic	Cahill	Terry(c)	Azpilcueta	Zouma	Matic
Wed 29	Leicester City	A	3-1	32,021	80	1	4-2-3-1	Cech	Ivanovic	Cahill	Terry(c)	Azpilcueta	Fàbregas	Matic
May														
Sun 3	Crystal Palace	H	1-0	41,566	83	1	4-2-3-1	Courtois	Ivanovic	Cahill	Terry(c)	Azpilicueta	Fàbregas	Matic
Sun 10	Liverpool	H	1-1	41,547	84	1	4-2-3-1	Courtois	Ivanovic	Zouma	Terry(c)	Filipe Luis	Loftus-Cheek	Matic
Mon 18	West Bromwich Albion	A	0-3	24,750	84	1	4-2-3-1	Courtois	Ivanovic	Cahill	Terry(c)	Filipe Luis	Loftus-Cheek	Mikel
Sun 24	Sunderland	H	3-1	41,620	87	1	4-2-3-1	Cech	Ivanovic	Cahill	Terry	Azpilicueta	Mikel	Matic

Chelsea score shown first. N - Neutral venue. UCL - UEFA Champions League. COC - Capital One Cup. FAC - FA Cup.
*Chelsea won 2-1 on aggregate after extra-time. •3-3 on aggregate after extra-time, Chelsea lost on away goals.

				Substitutes						
ürrle●	Oscar	Hazard	Diego Costa●■	Filipe Luis	Zouma	Mikel(82)	Willian(77)	Drogba(83)	Torres	Cech
ürrle	Oscar	Hazard●	Diego Costa●	Filipe Luis	Zouma	Mikel	Ramires(63)	Willian(69)	Drogba(79)	Cech
lian	Fàbregas■	Hazard	Diego Costa●●■	Filipe Luis(82)	Zouma	Mikel(74)	Schürrle	Salah	Drogba(88)	Cech
ürrle	Oscar	Hazard	Diego Costa●●●	Filipe Luis	Zouma	Ramires(h/t)	Willian	Salah(81)	Remy(72)●	Cech
lian	Fàbregas●	Hazard	Drogba	Azpilicueta	Zouma	Mikel	Oscar(67)	Diego Costa(74)	Remy(74)	Cech
mires■	Willian	Hazard	Diego Costa■	Filipe Luis	Mikel(62)	Oscar	Schürrle(62)●	Drogba(85)	Remy	Cech
ah	Oscar●	Schürrle	Remy	Ivanovic	Christensen	Matic(90+1)	Baker	Hazard(79)	Drogba(72)	Schwarzer
lian●	Oscar●	Hazard	Diego Costa●	Filipe Luis	Zouma	Mikel(77)	Schürrle(68)	Drogba	Remy(80)	Cech
ürrle	Oscar	Hazard■	Diego Costa	Azpilicueta	Zouma	Mikel(71)	Salah(84)	Willian(57)	Remy	Cech
ürrle■	Oscar■	Hazard●	Diego Costa●	Filipe Luis	Zouma	Mikel(69)	Salah	Willian(87)	Remy	Cech(24)
llian	Oscar●	Hazard	Remy	Filipe Luis(41)	Zouma	Mikel	Salah(86)	Drogba(90)	Solanke	Cech
llian	Oscar	Hazard●●	Remy●	Azpilicueta	Cahill	Ake(59)	Salah	Drogba(15)●	Solanke(72)	Courtois
llian	Oscar■	Hazard■	Drogba●■	Zouma(90+2)	Mikel(66)	Ake	Salah	Schürrle(89)	Baker	Cech
ah	Oscar	Schürrle	Drogba(c)●	Terry	Matic(79)	Willian(79)	Hazard(90+3)	Brown	Baker	Schwarzer
llian	Oscar●	Hazard●	Diego Costa	Zouma	Ake	Ramires(90+2)	Salah	Schürrle(77)	Drogba(63)	Cech
ürrle	Willian	Hazard	Drogba	Azpilicueta	Cahill	Ramires(55)	Salah	Oscar(h/t)	Diego Costa(h/t)	Courtois
mires	Oscar■	Hazard	Diego Costa■●	Filipe Luis(90+5)	Zouma	Mikel	Willian(54)	Drogba(89)	Remy	Cech
llian■	Oscar	Hazard●	Diego Costa●	Filipe Luis	Zouma	Ramires(86)	Schürrle	Drogba(83)	Remy(79)	Cech
llian●	Oscar	Hazard	Diego Costa	Filipe Luis	Zouma	Mikel	Ramires(75)●	Schürrle(78)	Drogba(66)●	Cech
llian	Oscar	Hazard	Diego Costa■	Filipe Luis	Zouma	Mikel	Schürrle(84)	Drogba(76)	Remy(76)	Cech
llian	Oscar	Hazard●	Drogba●	Filipe Luis	Zouma(h/t)	Mikel(76)	Schürrle	Salah	Remy(67)●	Cech
llian	Oscar	Hazard	Diego Costa■	Filipe Luis(67)	Zouma	Ramires	Schürrle(60)■	Drogba(67)●	Remy	Cech
hürrle●	Fàbregas●	Salah	Diego Costa	Ivanovic	Loftus-Cheek(83)	Ramires(74)	Oscar	Drogba	Remy(71)	Beeney
llian	Oscar	Hazard●	Diego Costa■●	Azpilicueta	Zouma	Ramires(81)	Schürrle(79)	Drogba(78)	Remy	Schwarzer
hürrle■●	Fàbregas	Hazard●	Drogba	Ivanovic(45+3)	Ramires(83)	Salah	Willian	Diego Costa	Remy(62)	Schwarzer
llian	Fàbregas●	Hazard	Diego Costa	Filipe Luis	Zouma(90+3)	Ake	Schürrle(79)	Oscar	Drogba(84)	Cech
llian	Oscar	Hazard	Diego Costa●	Filipe Luis	Zouma	Mikel(82)	Ramires(85)	Schürrle	Drogba(82)	Cech
hürrle	Fàbregas■	Hazard●	Diego Costa	Azpilicueta	Zouma	Ramires	Willian(h/t)	Drogba(74)	Remy(88)	Cech
llian	Oscar	Hazard●	Diego Costa●	Zouma	Mikel	Ramires(h/t)	Salah(72)	Drogba	Remy	Cech
hürrle	Oscar	Remy●	Drogba(c)	Ivanovic	Ake(79)	Matic	Salah	Willian(h/t)●	Diego Costa(h/t)	Courtois
illian	Oscar■	Hazard	Diego Costa●	Cahill	Filipe Luis(37)	Mikel	Ramires(78)	Drogba	Remy(83)	Courtois
illian	Oscar●●	Hazard	Diego Costa●●	Zouma	Mikel	Ramires(74)	Salah	Schürrle(76)●	Remy(74)	Courtois
illian	Fàbregas	Hazard●	Diego Costa	Azpilicueta(88)	Zouma	Ramires	Oscar	Drogba	Remy	Cech
emy	Oscar	Salah	Drogba(c)	Terry	Loftus-Cheek	Ake	Fàbregas(70)	Willian(69)	Hazard(76)	Courtois
illian	Oscar■	Hazard	Diego Costa■	Cahill	Azpilicueta(78)	Ake	Ramires(49)	Drogba(118)	Remy	Cech
illian	Oscar	Hazard	Remy●	Cahill(86)	Christensen	Ake	Loftus-Cheek(90+2)	Drogba(80)	Brown	Cech
illian	Oscar	Hazard●	Drogba	Zouma	Mikel(73)	Ake	Loftus-Cheek	Cuadrado(79)	Remy(64)	Cech
uadrado	Willian●	Hazard	Remy	Cahill(90+2)	Filipe Luis	Ake	Loftus-Cheek	Fàbregas(70)■	Drogba(70)	Courtois
illian	Fàbregas■	Hazard	Diego Costa	Filipe Luis	Zouma	Oscar(83)	Cuadrado(78)	Drogba	Remy(81)	Cech
uadrado	Oscar	Hazard	Diego Costa	Cahill	Azpilicueta	Ramires(71)	Willian(62)	Drogba(85)	Remy	Cech
àbregas	Willian■	Diego Costa●	Hazard	Filipe Luis	Ake	Oscar(88)	Cuadrado(75)■	Drogba(90+2)	Remy	Courtois
amires	Oscar	Hazard●■	Diego Costa	Filipe Luis	Loftus-Cheek	Willian(73)	Cuadrado	Drogba(90+3)	Remy(90+5)	Cech
amires■	Oscar■	Hazard●	Diego Costa	Filipe Luis	Zouma(84)	Willian(h/t)	Cuadrado	Drogba(f/t)	Remy	Cech
illian	Oscar	Hazard	Diego Costa●	Filipe Luis	Zouma	Ramires(53)	Cuadrado(83)	Drogba	Remy(81)	Cech
illian	Fàbregas	Hazard●	Diego Costa●	Azpilicueta	Zouma(79)	Loftus-Cheek	Cuadrado	Oscar(60)	Remy(75)●	Cech
illian	Oscar	Hazard●	Remy●	Filipe Luis	Zouma	Ramires	Cuadrado(63)	Diego Costa(h/t)	Drogba(56)■	Cech
àbregas●	Willian	Drogba■	Hazard	Filipe Luis	Zouma(90+1)	Mikel	Cuadrado(80)	Brown	Oscar(55)	Cech
scar■	Fàbregas	Hazard●	Drogba■	Filipe Luis	Mikel(90+2)	Ramires(67)	Willian(90+3)	Cuadrado	Solanke	Cech
amires	Willian■	Hazard	Oscar	Filipe Luis	Zouma(90)	Mikel	Loftus-Cheek	Cuadrado(90+3)	Drogba(h/t)	Cech
amires●	Willian	Hazard	Drogba●	Filipe Luis	Zouma(83)	Mikel(90)	Ake	Cuadrado(88)	Oscar	Courtois
uadrado	Willian	Hazard●	Drogba	Filipe Luis(90+2)	Zouma(84)	Mikel(h/t)	Ake	Loftus-Cheek	Remy	Cech
illian	Fàbregas■	Hazard	Remy	Cahill(34)	Azpilicueta	Matic(60)	Ake	Cuadrado(83)	Drogba	Beeney
emy	Fàbregas■(28)	Hazard	Diego Costa■	Azpilicueta	Christensen	Mikel	Ake(72)	Cuadrado(63)■	Brown(79)	Blackman
uadrado■	Willian	Hazard	Drogba(c)	Filipe Luis	Christensen(78)	Boga	Diego Costa(29)●	Remy(43)●●	Solanke	Courtois

Own goals (4): Coleman, Everton (A), Viler, Maribor (H), Grandison, Shrewsbury Town (A). Kirchhoff, Schalke (A).
Penalties (9): Hazard 6, Drogba 1, Fàbregas 1. Diego Costa 1.

THE TROPHY GOES ON TOUR

There's no point in having a lovely trinket and keeping it all to yourself, so a bank holiday Monday was made all the more special as the Chelsea squad took the Premier League trophy to the streets of west London...

CHAMPIONS
2014/15
CHELSEA
FOOTBALL CLUB

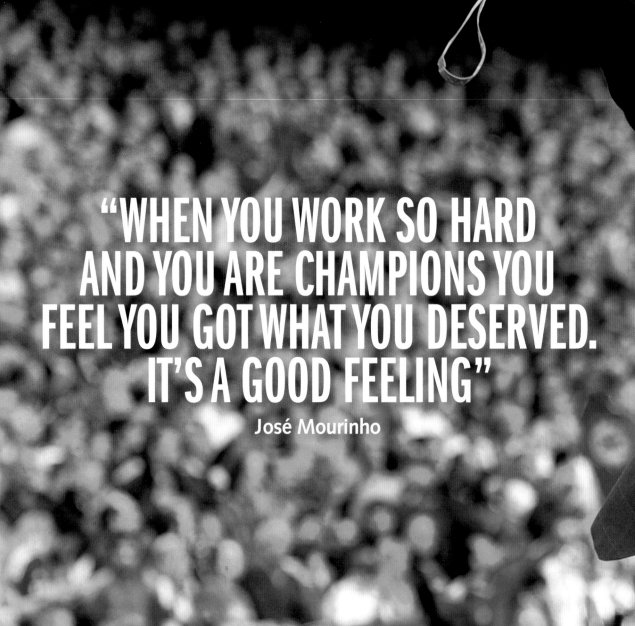

"WHEN YOU WORK SO HARD
AND YOU ARE CHAMPIONS YOU
FEEL YOU GOT WHAT YOU DESERVED.
IT'S A GOOD FEELING"

José Mourinho